Baking Magic

with Serafina the Unicorn Baker

30 SWEET AND SPECTACULAR RECIPES

Serafina Alessi

Copyright © 2023 by Serafina Alessi

All rights reserved. This book or any portion thereof may not be reproduced or used in any manner whatsoever without the express written permission of the author.

To all the little bakers out there who love to create magic in the kitchen, this book is for you. May you find joy, happiness, and inspiration in every recipe you bake!

Acknowledgements

A special thank you to my sister Lucy, brother Luca, Mom and Dad, Grandparents, and friends for their love and support throughout my baking journey. You guys are the best!

Thanks to all my friends in the baking community for being so awesome and inspiring! Your creativity and love for baking have inspired me so much and I'm so grateful to share my recipes with you.

And finally, a huge thank you to all my fans and subscribers! Your support and encouragement have made all my baking dreams come true. You guys rock!

Thank you!
Serafina the Unicorn Baker

Table of Contents

Introduction: Welcome to Serafina the Unicorn Baker's Kitchen..................1

CHAPTER 1: SWEET TREATS FOR KIDS

1. Healthy Protein Muffins!..................2
2. Vanilla Bomb Ice Cream Hot Chocolate..................4
3. Fun Gingerbread House..................6
4. 4th of July Strawberry Parfait..................8
5. M&M Pretzel Chocolate Hugs & Kisses..................10

CHAPTER 2: WAFFLES & CAKES

6. Healthy Protein Waffles..................12
7. 1 Minute Microwave Unicorn Mug Cake..................14
8. Rainbow Unicorn Dump Cake!..................16
9. S'mores Mini Waffles..................18
10. Funfetti Unicorn Cake..................20
11. Chocolate Mini Donuts..................22
12. Valentine's Day Chocolate Covered Strawberries..................24

CHAPTER 3: CUPCAKES, COOKIES & BROWNIES

13. Reese's Stuffed Peanut Butter Cupcakes..................26
14. Baketivity Red Velvet Cupcakes..................28
15. Baketivity Gingerbread Men Cookies..................30
16. Baketivity Jumbo Yum&M Cookies..................32
17. Cadbury Birds Nest Cookies..................34

18. White Chocolate Oreo Fudge 36
19. Tres Leches Cake 38
20. Baketivity Classic Snowball Cookies 40
21. Pillsbury Funfetti Holiday Cake Mix Sugar Cookies 42
22. Baketivity Pretty Petals Cookies 44
23. Sea Salt Caramel Brownies 46
24. Chocolate Peanut Butter Brownies 48

CHAPTER 4: SMOOTHIES & SNACKS
25. Strawberry Vanilla Banana Smoothies 50
26. Halloween Scarecrow Snack Mix 52
27. Cream Cheese Marshmallow Fluff Fruit Dip 54
28. At-Home Disney Dole Whip 56
29. Scary Halloween Protein Pancakes 58
30. Oatmeal Breakfast Cups 60

CONCLUSION: 62

Introduction

Hi Friends!

I'm Serafina the Unicorn Baker and I'm super excited to share my baking adventures with you! I'm 11 years old and I have a huge passion for two things - unicorns and baking! Baking is so much fun and it brings me so much joy to see families come together and have fun in the kitchen. That's why I wanted to create this book with yummy and easy-to-make recipes that you can bake with your kids, family, or friends.

In this book, you'll find 30 delicious baking treats that I've made myself and that I just know you'll love! I've put my heart and soul into each recipe and I can't wait for you to try them all. There's cookies, baked goods, holiday favorites, and even some snacks that are perfect for any time of day.

So, put on your apron, grab your baking ingredients, and let's get started! Get ready to have some fun and learn some new baking skills on this magical baking journey.

Also, please remember to subscribe to my YouTube channel:

Serafina the Unicorn Baker - Unicorns, Baking & Rainbows
@serafinatheunicornbaker

SWEET TREATS FOR KIDS

1

Makes 6 muffins

Healthy Protein Muffins!

It's good and healthy for you and you can eat it for breakfast. Also, you can eat it on a holiday for fewer calories! It will taste good if it's either hot or cold outside. And my brother Luca said it does not taste dry!

Use Whey Protein Isolate ~ they bake the best!

Ingredients

4	Eggs
4 Scoops	Chocolate or Vanilla Protein powder
2 Cups	Protein Pancake Powder

You Will Need
- Mixing Bowl
- Large Fork
- Large Spoon
- Silicone Muffin Mold

Instructions

1. Crack four eggs into a mixing bowl
2. Add four scoops of Protein Powder into the mixing bowl
3. Add two cups of Protein Pancake Powder into the mixing bowl
4. Mix the ingredients with a large fork
5. Add water as necessary to create a pancake batter consistency
6. Using the large spoon, begin filling the silicone muffin mold
7. Place silicone muffin mold into the microwave for two minutes on high
8. Pop the muffins out of the mold and place them on a dish

   Serve and enjoy!

Serafina Alessi

SWEET TREATS FOR KIDS

2

Makes 2 servings

Vanilla Bomb Ice Cream Hot Chocolate

If you just come out of the snow or if it's a cold day, you should drink it to warm-up. It's kind of like a little dessert that you could have. It's like lemonade but for the winter!

Ingredients

2 Packets	SwissMiss Hot Chocolate Mix
4 Cups	Hot Water
2 Scoops	French Vanilla Ice Cream

You Will Need

- Hot Chocolate Mugs
- 2 Spoons
- Ice Cream Scoop

Instructions

1. Empty a packet of hot chocolate mix into each of the mugs
2. Place 4 cups of hot water into a micorwave for 2 minutes to bring water to a boil
3. Carefully pour the hot water into the mugs with the hot chocolate mix
4. Stir contents until all the hot chocolate is dissolved
5. Scoop french vanilla ice cream into the hot chocolate

   Serve and enjoy!

Baking Magic with Serafina the Unicorn Baker   5

Fun Gingerbread House

During the holidays this is fun to make. When people come over you can ask them to grade it. When you're done with it and only then, can you eat it! It's a lot of sugar so be careful!!

Makes 1 gingerbread house

Ingredients

1	Gingerbread House
1/2 Cup	Royal Icing
1/2 Cup	Christmas Sprinkles
???	Edible Christmas Decorations

You Will Need
- Large sheet or base
- Piping bag
- Spoon

Instructions

1 Set the gingerbread house on a solid base

2 Glue the sides of the house together with royal icing

3 Using a piping bag, pipe a thick line of icing along a short end of the side pieces

4 Using the sprinkles and decorations, decorate and have fun!

Serve and enjoy!

Serafina Alessi

Baking Magic with Serafina the Unicorn Baker

SWEET TREATS FOR KIDS

4

Makes 16 servings

4th of July Strawberry Parfait

The perfect dessert to celebrate Independence Day, or any American Holiday! Moms will let us kids eat this dessert more often because it has fruit in it!

Ingredients

1 Box	Pillsbury Moist Supreme Cake Mix
8 oz	Blueberries
8 oz	Strawberries
1 Cup	Cool Whip

You Will Need
- 9 x 13" baking pan
- Cutting Board
- Glass Mixing Bowls
- Spatula
- Knife
- Clear Plastic Cups

Instructions

1. Bake the cake, following instructions on the box
2. Cut the strawberries into small chunks and add to a glass mixing bowl
3. Cut the cake into small squares and place the cake into the plastic cups
4. Scoop 1-2 tablespoons of blueberries into each cup
5. Scoop a layer of cool whip on top of the blueberries
6. Scoop strawberries into each cup
7. Repeat with cool whip, blueberries and strawberries until the cups are full and they look red, white and blue!

Serve and enjoy!

Serafina Alessi

SWEET TREATS FOR KIDS

5

Makes 4-6 servings

M&M Pretzel Chocolate Hugs & Kisses

This is great for Christmas to give it to family or friends or even yourself. It is also good to give to Santa Claus! It's pretty easy to make but be sure it has cooled down before you eat it ~ as I burned my mouth!

Ingredients

1 Pack	Bite-sized Pretzel twists or squares
1 Cup	Hershey's Kisses ~ plain
1 Cup	Hershey's Kisses ~ mint
1 Cup	M&M's ~ peanut
1 Cup	M&M's ~ plain

You Will Need
- Cookie sheet
- 4 Small bowls
- Parchment paper

Instructions

1. Preheat the oven to 350°F. Place parchment paper on a cookie sheet
2. Place pretzel squares on parchment paper, evenly spaced and close together
3. Pour plain and mint Hershey's kisses into two separate bowls
4. Unwrap the kisses and place one Hershey's kisses on each pretzel square
5. Place the tray of pretzel squares into the oven for a few minutes, just enough to melt the kisses
6. Pour plain and peanut M&M's into separate bowls
7. Remove the pretzels from the oven, and gently press one M&M into the melted chocolate

Serve and enjoy!

Healthy Protein Waffles

I love waffles but they are not always the healthiest. This is a healthier way to have waffles so that you can enjoy them more often!

Makes 4 waffles

Ingredients

2	Eggs
4 Tbsp	Almond Flour
4 Scoops	Chocolate Protein Powder
1 Tbsp	Butter

You Will Need
- Waffle mold
- Measuring bowl
- Spoon
- Whisk

Instructions

1. Crack two eggs into a measuring bowl
2. Add 4 tablespoons of almond flour into the measuring bowl
3. Add 4 scoops of protein powder into the bowl
4. Whisk the mixture, and add a splash of water if necessary
5. Carefully pour mixture into the waffle mold evenly
6. Microwave on high for two minutes. Carefully remove, it will be hot!
7. Add butter on top of the waffles

Serve and enjoy!

Serafina Alessi

WAFFLES AND CAKES

7

Makes 3 servings

1 Minute Microwave Unicorn Mug Cake

If you eat this it is probably a lot of calories but it's worth it! It tastes amazingly good because it comes from a Unicorn!

Ingredients

3 Packets	Rainbow Mug Treats Mug Cake Mix
9 Tbps	Unsweetened Almond Milk (divided)
	Frosting

You Will Need
- 3 Mugs
- Whisk
- Tablespoon
- Fork

Instructions

1 Empty one pack of mug cake mix into each cup

2 Into each cup, add 3 tablespoons of unsweetened almond milk. Using the whisk, stir to combine well until the cake mix is dissolved

3 Microwave on high for one minute. The mug will be hot, so be careful taking it out of the microwave!

4 Add frosting

Serve and enjoy!

Serafina Alessi

WAFFLES AND CAKES

8

Rainbow Unicorn Dump Cake

When you add the sprinkles make sure not to make a big mess. But, it's worth it in the end because it's delicious!

Makes 1 9x13" cake

Ingredients

1 Cup	Unsweetened Almond Milk
1 Box	Party Rainbow Cake Mix
1 Pack	Golden Oreo Cookies
1 Box	Vanilla Pudding Mix
8 oz Pack	White Chocolate Chips
1 Stick	Butter
1/2 Cup	Rainbow Sprinkles

You Will Need

- 9 x 13" Baking pan
- Measuring cups
- Whisk
- Spatula
- Fork

Instructions

1. Preheat the oven to 350°F

2. In the measuring cup, pour one cup of unsweetened almond milk, and pudding mix. Whisk to combine

3. Pour the mixture into the baking pan and smooth out with a spatula.

4. Set 8 golden Oreo cookies aside, then line the remainder on the pan, 1/4" apart

5. Sprinkle white chocolate chips over the top of the cookies

6. Dump the Party Rainbow Chip cake mix over the top of the other ingredients and smooth out with a fork

7. Cut butter into small cubes and place them on top of the mixture, spacing them 1/2" apart

Serafina Alessi

8	Place eight golden Oreo cookies in a ziplock bag and crush with a rolling pin
9	Sprinkle crushed oreos on top of the mixture
10	Add sprinkles to the top of the cake
11	Bake for 20 minutes, then let it cool down
12	Cut it into squares

Serve and enjoy!

WAFFLES AND CAKES 9

Makes 2 servings

S'mores Mini Waffles

This is more fun than Grandpa's Oatmeal (inside joke)! I love it on the weekend for a breakfast treat!

I like topping my waffles with additional melted chocolate and mini marshmallows, so make sure you have a little extra!

Ingredients

3/4 Cup	Graham Cracker Crumbs
2 Tsp	White Sugar
1 1/2 Tsp	Baking Powder
1	Egg
2/5 Cup	Whole Milk
2 Tbsp	Mini Chocolate Chips
1 1/4 Cup	Mini Marshmallows
A little	Macadamia Nut Oil

You Will Need

- 2 Mixing Bowls
- Mini Waffle Maker
- Whisk
- Spatula
- Measuring Spoons
- Cups

Instructions

1. In a small mixing bowl, combine graham cracker crumbs, sugar and baking powder

2. In a separate mixing bowl, crack an egg, add milk and whisk together

3. Fold the dry ingredients into the wet ingredients and stir to combine

4. Add the mini chocolate chips and mini marshmallows and stir gently

5. Spray the waffle maker with oil, and pour batter into the waffle maker

6. Close the top and let cook for two minutes

7. Carefully remove from the waffle maker and repeat until all the batter has been used

8. For a topping, add two tablespoons of chocolate chips into a small microwaveable bowl and microwave for 30 seconds

9. Spread melted chocolate on top of the waffle and add more mini marshmallows to decorate

Serve and enjoy!

Funfetti Unicorn Cake

This is perfect if you love Unicorns SOOOO MUCH!!!

Makes 1 9x13" cake

Ingredients

1 Box	Funfetti Cake Mix
1 Tub, 15 oz	Funfeti Vanilla Frosting with Unicorn Sprinkles
4	Eggs
1/4 Cup	Vegetable Oil
1 Cup	Water
	Non-stick Spray

You Will Need

- 9 x 13" Baking Pan
- Mixer or Beaters
- Whisk
- Spatula
- Spoon
- Measuring Cups

Instructions

1. Preheat the oven to 350°F
2. Empty the contents of the cake mix into the mixing bowl of a stand mixer
3. Add water and oil into the mixing bowl
4. Crack 4 eggs into the bowl
5. Mix on low speed for 2 minutes, then empty the mixture into a greased baking pan
6. Place into the oven and bake for 25 minutes
7. Once cool, frost and add sprinkles

   Cut, serve and enjoy!

Serafina Alessi

Baking Magic with Serafina the Unicorn Baker

WAFFLES AND CAKES 11

Chocolate Mini Donuts

If you've never tried donuts before, this is a great place to start! Also, they are small which is the perfect size for little kids. It's also a lot of fun using the donut maker!

Makes 14 mini donuts

🍴 Ingredients

2 Cups	Flour
1/4 Cup	Cocoa Powder
2 Tsp	Baking Powder
Pinch	Salt
1 Cup	Sugar
2	Eggs
1/3 Stick	Butter (melted)
2 Tbsp	Vanilla Extract
1/3 Cup	Sour Cream
A little	Oil (Macadamia Nut Oil)

Frosting

1 1/2 Cups	Powdered Sugar
4 Tbsp	Baking Powder
1/3 Cup	Half-and-half
2 Tbsp	Vanilla Extract
1/2 Cup	Chocolate Sprinkles

You Will Need
- 3 Mixing Bowls
- Whisk
- Spatula
- Dash Donut Maker
- Toothpicks

Instructions

1. Mix the flour, cocoa powder, baking powder and salt into a mixing bowl

2. In another bowl, mix the eggs, sugar, vanilla extract, milk, melted butter and sour cream. Whisk to combine

Serafina Alessi

3. Fold the dry ingredients into the wet ingredients, adding a little at a time and mixing until fully combined. Whisk until it becomes batter consistency

4. Spray the donut maker with oil, then spoon the batter into the donut maker

5. Close the lid and let it cook for 90 seconds, then flip with a toothpick and close the lid for another 90 seconds

6. Carefully remove the donuts to a cooling rack and repeat until all the batter is cooked. Let all the donuts cool completely

7. To prepare the frosting, mix together the cocoa powder, flour, vanilla extract and half-and-half into a medium sized mixing bowl

8. Use a spatula to frost the donuts, then top with some chocolate sprinkles

Serve and enjoy!

WAFFLES AND CAKES

12

Makes 4 servings

Valentine's Day Chocolate Covered Strawberries

You should eat this for Valentines Day as it makes a great dessert!

Ingredients

1 Pound Pack	Strawberries
1 Cup	Chocolate Wafers
1/2 Cup	Valentine's Sprinkles
1/2 Cup	Rice Krispies Crispy Rice Cereal

You Will Need
- Crock Pot
- Strainers
- Glass Bowl
- 2 Plates
- Tablespoon
- Teaspoon
- Spatula
- Wax Paper

Instructions

1. Place parchment paper on a plate
2. Using a strainer, give the strawberries a good wash, then dry them thoroughly
3. Turn on the crock pot and let it come up to temperature
4. Place 1 cup of chocolate wafers into the crock pot to melt and stir gradually
5. Pour Valentines sprinkles into a glass bowl
6. Pour Rice Krispies into a separate bowl
7. Once the chocolate has melted, take one strawberry at a time, and dip into the chocolate, then coat with sprinkles and place on the parchment paper

8. To make use of the leftover chocolate, stir Rice Krispies into the melted chocolate in the crock pot

9. Using a spoon, scoop chocolate mixture onto a plate lined with parchment paper

10. Place the chocolates into the refrigerator to chill

11. Once they are cool and solid, remove from refrigerator and put them on a plate

Serve and enjoy!

CUPCAKES, COOKIES AND BROWNIES

13

Makes 12 cupcakes

Reese's Stuffed Peanut Butter Cupcakes

This dessert is really good for anyone who loves chocolate and peanut butter! Make sure that you don't over-bake it because no one likes it burnt!

Ingredients

12	Reese's Cups
1 Box	Pillsbury Chocolate Fudge Brownie Mix
1/3 Cup	Vegetable Oil
1/4 Cup	Water
2	Eggs

You Will Need
- Cupcake Liners
- Cupcake Baking Tray
- Measuring Cups
- Mixing Bowl
- Spatula
- Spoon

Instructions

1 Preheat the oven to 350° F

2 Place 12 Reese's Cups into a mixing bowl

3 Open box of Pillsbury Chocolate Fudge Brownie Mix and pour into a glass bowl

4 Add oil and water to the brownie mix

5 Crack two eggs into the mixture, then stir to combine

6 Place cupcake liners into the baking tray

7 Using a measuring cup, scoop the mixture into each cupcake liner

8 Bake for 20 minutes, then remove and let cool. Place onto a fancy container

Serve and enjoy!

Serafina Alessi

CUPCAKES, COOKIES AND BROWNIES

14

Baketivity Red Velvet Cupcakes

This is perfect for Valentine's Day! If you see these candies on top you don't have to melt them ~ just place them on top and eat!

Makes 10 cupcakes

Ingredients

1 Box	Baketivity Red Velvet Cupcakes
2/3 Cup	Cooking oil
4 + 2 Tbsp	Almond Milk (divided)
2	Eggs
1 Tsp	White vinegar
1 Stick	Butter, softened

You Will Need
- Cupcake Baking Tray
- Cupcake Liners
- 3 Mixing Bowls
- Spoon
- Ice Cream Scoop

Instructions

1. Preheat the oven to 350°F
2. Unpack the Baketivity Red Velvet Cupcakes box
3. Line the cupcake baking tray with cupcake liner
4. Whisk flour, cocoa, baking soda and salt packets from the Baketivity box
5. In a separate bowl, whisk 1/2 cup oil, sugar and vanilla from the Baketivity box
6. Add four teaspoons of almond milk and crack two eggs into the mixture
7. Add the food dye packet and a teaspoon of vinegar into the mixture and whisk to combine

Serafina Alessi

Follow along in this video!

8   Slowly add the dry ingredients into the wet ingredients and whisk together

9   Using an ice cream scoop, scoop the batter into the cupcake liner, filling 3/4 of the way to the top

10   Place into the oven and bake for 20 minutes

11   In the meantime, let's make the frosting! In a mixing bowl, add one stick of softened butter, 1 packet of confectioner's sugar and 3 tablespoons of almond milk and whisk until creamy

12   Remove cupcakes from oven and let stand to cool

13   Once cupcakes are cool, place on a serving tray

14   Scoop frosting mixture into the Baketivity piping bag and squeeze icing on top of the cupcakes, and top with strawberry wafers from the Baketivity set

Serve and enjoy!

CUPCAKES, COOKIES AND BROWNIES

15

Makes 12-15 cookies

Baketivity Gingerbread Men Cookies

This is perfect for the holidays. I had trouble with the frosting so some of them came out smeared - but that's okay. They still taste great!

Ingredients

1 Box	Baketivity Gingerbread Men Box
1	Egg
1/8 Cup	Cooking Oil
6 Tbsp	Water

You Will Need

- Cookie Sheet
- Parchment Paper
- Tablespoon
- Stand Mixer
- Teaspoon
- Rolling PIn
- Whisk
- Mixing Bowl

Instructions

1. For the cookies: whisk together the flour, ginger, cinnamon, baking soda, salt, allspice and cloves in a large bowl

2. Mix the egg, brown sugar and vanilla sugar in the bowl of a stand mixer fitted with the paddle attachment.

3. Gradually beat the dry ingredients into the wet ingredients in two additions

4. Divide the dough in half, roll to 1/2 inch thick, wrap in plastic wrap and refrigerate for 2 hours

5. Preheat the oven to 350°F

6. On a lightly floured surface, roll out one piece of dough to 1/4 inch thick. Cut to 3-5 inch cookies with a gingerbread man cutter or desired shape. Brush off any excess flour.

Serafina Alessi

Follow along in this video!

6. Repeat with remaining dough, lining cookies on a parchment-lined cookie sheet and refrigerate for 15 minutes.

7. Bake in batches until they are golden around the edges, 12 to 15 minutes

8. Transfer to a wire rack and let cool completely

9. For the royal icing, whisk the confectioner's sugar with the powdered sugar in the bowl of a stand mixer fitted with the paddle attachment

10. Beat in 6 Tbsp of water until very well combined and the icing forms stiff glossy peaks. Add 1 Tbsp water at a time until you have a smooth pipeable consistency. Add in food coloring if desired

11. Fill pastry bags fitted with tips and decorate the gingerbread cookies with the icing

Serve and enjoy!

Baking Magic with Serafina the Unicorn Baker

CUPCAKES, COOKIES AND BROWNIES

16

Baketivity Jumbo Yum&M Cookies

If you love to bake and want to share a treat with a friend, this is the perfect cookie! By the way, who doesn't love M&M's - right?

Makes 2 cookies

Ingredients

1 Box	Baketivity Jumbo M&M Cookies Kit
1 Stick	Butter (at room temperature)
1	Egg (large)

You Will Need
- 2 Cookie Sheets
- 2 Mixing Bowls
- Parchment Paper
- Whisk
- Silicone Spatula
- Scoop or Spoon
- Cooling Rack

Instructions

1. Preheat the oven to 350°F

2. Line 2 cookie sheets with parchment paper, or silicone baking mats. Set aside

3. In a medium mixing bowl, combine the flour, baking soda and salt. Set aside

4. In a large mixing bowl, whisk 1 stick of softened (almost melted) butter, until it is smooth and creamy

5. To the butter, add the brown sugar and sugar. Continue to whisk until the mixture is smooth. Use a spatula to scrape the mixture if it gets stuck in the whisk

6. Add 1 egg and vanilla sugar and whisk until it is smooth

7. Add in your dry ingredients and use your silicone spatula to combine. Continue mixing until your dough is just combined

8. Fold in the chocolate M&Ms until they are evenly distributed in your dough. Set some M&Ms aside to place on top of the cookies!

9. Using a scoop or spoon, scoop roughly 3 Tbsp-sized balls. These are jumbo cookies so the dough balls should be large!

10. Place the cookie dough balls on the lined cookie sheet about 2 inches apart. Add 2-3 M&Ms on top of the cookies

11. Bake 13-14 minutes, or until golden brown

12. Remove cookies from the oven and let them sit for 1-2 minutes. Then, transfer them to a cooling rack to cool completely

Serve and enjoy!

CUPCAKES, COOKIES AND BROWNIES

17

Cadbury Birds Nest Cookies

This is perfect if you love birds! This is also a great dessert for Easter and the spring time!

Makes 15 cookies

Ingredients

- Milk Chocolate Chips
- Reese's Peanut Butter Chocolate Chips
- Cadbury Mini Eggs
- Chow Mein Noodles

You Will Need

- Silicone Muffin Mold
- Mixing Bowls
- Spatula
- Spoon
- Muffin Liners

Instructions

1. Place milk chocolate chips and Reese's peanut butter chocolate chips in a large microwaveable bowl

2. Place in the microwave for 45 to 60 seconds until softened, then stir. Microwave in short bursts if not softened

3. Mix the chow mein noodles into the bowl

4. Place baking liners into the silicon muffin mold and fill each liner 1/2 of the way

5. Place 3 Cadbury Mini Eggs on top of each nest cookie in the mold

6. Refrigerate for 15 minutes to cool, then remove from the mold and serve on a plate

Serve and enjoy!

CUPCAKES, COOKIES AND BROWNIES

18

Makes 1 8x8" tray

White Chocolate Oreo Fudge

This is a delicious dessert on a hot summer day. If you love Oreos so, so much like I do, put a lot in! But remember to crunch them all up into small pieces!!

Use the highest quality white chocolate that you would enjoy eating on its own. Chocolate is the main ingredient, so quality and flavor is everything!

Ingredients

14 oz	High-quality White Chocolate wafers or chips
1 Tsp	Vanilla Extract
1 Can	Sweetened Condensed Milk
1 Pack	Oreo Cookies

You Will Need
- 2 Microwaveable Mixing Bowls
- Parchment Paper
- 8 x 8" Baking Pan
- Spatula

Instructions

1. Break Oreos into 1/4 size pieces in a glass mixing bowl. Set aside

2. In a microwaveable glass bowl, add 12-14 oz white chocolate wafers or chips

3. Place the white chocolate in the microwave for 20-second intervals until melted

4. Once melted and smooth, add 1 teaspoon vanilla extract, and 1 can of swetened condensed milk. Stir to combine

5. Add the Oreo pieces and fold to combine using a spatula

6. Line a baking pan with parchment paper, then add the mixture to the pan

7. Add additional Oreo pieces on top of the mixture, then place in the refrigerator to cool completely.

Serve and enjoy!

Serafina Alessi

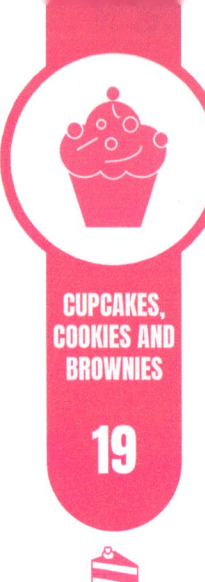

CUPCAKES, COOKIES AND BROWNIES

19

Makes 1 9x13" cake

Tres Leches Cake

Perfect for Cinco de Mayo or anytime you are feeling a little festive!

Ingredients

1 Box	Vanilla Cake Mix
3	Eggs
1 Cup	Water
1/2 Cup	Neutral Oil
2 Cups	Milk
1 Can	Sweetened Condensed Milk
1 Can	Evaporated Milk
1 Tub	Whipped Topping

You Will Need
- 9 x 13" Cake Pan
- Mixing Bowls
- Whisk
- Measuring Cups
- Fork
- Aluminum Foil

Instructions

1. Preheat the oven to 350°F

2. Grease a 9" by 13" cake pan

3. Into a large mixing bowl, add 1 cup of water, 1/2 cup of oil and the package contents of cake mix. Crack 3 eggs into the bowl

4. Using a whisk, mix to combine

5. Pour mixture into the greased cake pan, and shake the pan gently to release air bubbles

6. Bake in the oven for 30 minutes

7. Remove from the oven and let the cake cool for 1 hour

Serafina Alessi

8   Once the cake has cooled completely, use a fork to poke holes evenly across the cake, so that the milk can soak in!

9   In another mixing bowl, combine the milk, condensed milk and evaporated milk. Whisk to combine

10 Pour the milk mixture over the top of the cake

11 Cover the cake with tin foil and place in the fridge to cool for 2 hours or more

12 Top with whipped topping

Serve and enjoy!

CUPCAKES, COOKIES AND BROWNIES

20

Baketivity Classic Snowball Cookies

These are perfect on a cold, snowy winter day!

Makes 20 cookies

Ingredients

1 Box	Baketivity Snowball Cookie Kit
1/2 Cup	Butter

You Will Need
- Baking sheet
- Measuring cups
- Measuring spoons
- Glass bowls
- Whisk
- Ice cream scoop
- Spatula
- Parchment paper

Instructions

1 Preheat the oven to 375°F

2 Unpack the Baketivity Snowball Cookie kit

3 Line a baking sheet with parchment paper

4 Add 1/2 cup butter into a glass bowl

5 To the bowl, add the confectioner's sugar packet and vanilla sugar packet. Stir with a whisk until combined

6 Add flour packet and salt packet, and whisk again until combined. Refrigerate for 5 to 10 minutes

7 Add the sprinkle packet and stir

Serafina Alessi

8 Using an ice cream scoop, scoop out cookie-sized pieces of dough onto the baking sheet

9 Bake for 7 minutes, then let it cool for 5 minutes

10 While the cookies are baking, place the second packet of confectioner's sugar into a mixing bowl

11 Remove the cooled cookies from the baking sheet and dip them into the confectioner's sugar and coat evenly

12 Place on a serving dish

Serve and enjoy!

Baking Magic with Serafina the Unicorn Baker

CUPCAKES, COOKIES AND BROWNIES

21

Pillsbury Funfetti Holiday Cake Mix Sugar Cookies

Cake mix cookies are the ultimate no-hassle treat! I added sprinkles and frosting to mine. I also made a few extra to share with my friends and my teacher. I hope you like it!

Makes 20 cookies

Ingredients

1 Box	Pillsbury Funfetti Cake Mix
1/2 Cup	Vegetable Oil
1/3 Cup	Water
2	Eggs
1 15oz Tub	Frosting
???	Food Coloring
1 Package	Cookie Icing (to decorate)

You Will Need
- Cookie Sheet
- Large Mixing Bowl
- Measuring Cups
- Spoon
- Spatula

Instructions

1. Preheat the oven to 375°F
2. Open the Funfetti Cake Mix and dump contents into a large mixing bowl.
3. Add 1/2 cup vegetable oil and two eggs into the mixing bowl
4. Add water and stir thoroughly until the mixture has a cookie like consistency
5. Using a spoon, place mixture onto a cookie sheet in cookie-sized servings
6. Place cookies in oven and bake for 6-8 minutes
7. Remove cookies and allow them to cool for one minute before placing on a rack

Serafina Alessi

8. Once cooled completely, remove the cookies from the cooling rack and place on dishes
9. Frost the cookies
10. Using a spoon, add the cookie sprinkles
11. Add icing as desired for decoration

Serve and enjoy!

CUPCAKES, COOKIES AND BROWNIES

22

Makes 12-15 cookies

Baketivity Pretty Petals Cookies

This is perfect for a spring day treat. I love the flowers and I enjoyed packing them in my lunch for school!

Ingredients

1 Box	Baketivity Pretty Pedals Cookies Kit
1/2 Cup	Unsalted Butter, softened
1	Egg

You Will Need
- 2 Mixing Bowls
- Fork
- Whisk
- Measuring Cups
- Measuring Spoons
- 4 Small Bowls
- Parchment Paper
- 2 Baking Sheets

Instructions

1. Preheat the oven to 375°F

2. Line two baking sheets with parchment paper

3. In a small mixing bowl, whisk together flour, baking soda, baking powder and salt. Set aside

4. In another mixing bowl, mix together softened butter, sugar and egg

5. Fold the dry ingredients into the wet ingredients

6. Scoop dough in one teaspoon-sized balls and place on baking sheet

7. Pour each of the four colored sugar crystal packets into small serving bowls

Serafina Alessi

8   Coat each cookie ball with sugar crystals

9   Bake for 8 to 10 minutes until golden brown, then let cool

10   Add yellow chocolate wafers into a glasss mixing bowl and microwave until melted

11   Pour the melted yellow chocolate wafers into the middle of a cookie ball so that they look like a flower and flower petals

Serve and enjoy!

Baking Magic with Serafina the Unicorn Baker

CUPCAKES, COOKIES AND BROWNIES

23

Makes 1 9x12" tray

Sea Salt Caramel Brownies

If you love sea-salt caramel, peanut butter and brownies, this is the ultimate dessert for a sweet treat! My sister Lucy couldn't stop eating it!!

Ingredients

1/4 Cup	Water
2/3 Cup	Vegetable Oil
2	Eggs
1 Box	Pillsbury Chocolate Fudge Brownie Mix
10oz Pack	Sea Salt Caramel Baking Chips
	Cooking Spray
To serve	Light Caramel Swirl Ice Cream
To serve	Smuckers Simply Delicious Caramel Topping

You Will Need
- 9 x 12" Baking Pan
- 1 Mixing Bowl
- 2 Measuring Cups
- Spatula

Instructions

1. Preheat the oven to 350°F

2. Lightly grease the baking pan with vegetable oil cooking spray

3. In a large mixing bowl, add water, oil and eggs

4. Add the package contents of the brownie mix and stir to combine

5. Add a 10oz pack of sea salt caramel baking chips and stir

6. Pour mixture into the baking pan and bake for 30 minutes

7. Remove the brownies from the oven and let it cool, then cut into squares

   Serve with caramel swirl ice cream and caramel topping!

Serafina Alessi

Baking Magic with Serafina the Unicorn Baker

CUPCAKES, COOKIES AND BROWNIES

24

Makes 1 9x12" tray

Chocolate Peanut Butter Brownies

If you love brownies and chocolate, this is perfect. Also, I got some of this on my mouth and teeth so remember to brush afterwards!

Ingredients

1 Box	Chocolate Peanut Butter Brownie Mix
1/4 Cup	Vegetable Oil
2	Eggs
	Chocolate Frosting

You Will Need
- 9 x 12" Baking Pan
- Measuring Cups
- Spatula
- Glass Mixing Bowl

Instructions

1. Preheat the oven to 325°F
2. Add the chocolate peanut butter brownie mix into a mixing bowl
3. Add 1/4 cup of vegetable oil into the mixture
4. Crack 2 eggs into the mixture and stir to combine
5. Spray the baking pan with non-stick cooking spray
6. Add the brownie mixture to the baking pan and spread evenly with a spatula
7. Place into the oven and bake for 35 minutes
8. Allow the brownies to cool completely, around three hours
9. Frost the brownies, then cut and place onto a dish

Serve and enjoy!

SMOOTHIES AND SNACKS

25

Makes 3 smoothies

Strawberry Vanilla Banana Smoothies

This dessert is refreshing and healthy! I love it on a hot summer day. Super-easy to make and you get to use a blender!

Ingredients

2 Scoops	Vanilla Protein Powder
1/3 Cup	Greek Yoghurt
1 Cup	Almond Milk
4 oz	Strawberries
1	Banana
1 Cup	Ice Cubes

You Will Need
- Cutting Board
- Knife
- Spoon
- Measuring Cup
- Blender
- Large Plastic Cups with Straws

Instructions

1. Wash and cut strawberries into small chunks and put in blender
2. Peel and cut banana into small chunks and put in blender
3. Add 1/3 cup of greek yoghurt to the blender
4. Add 1 cup of almond milk into the blender
5. Add two scoops of vanilla protein powder into the blender
6. Add 1 cup of ice cubes into blender
7. Blend until smooth, then pour into large plastic cups

Serve and enjoy!

Serafina Alessi

Baking Magic with Serafina the Unicorn Baker 51

SMOOTHIES AND SNACKS

26

Makes 12 servings

Halloween Scarecrow Snack Mix

Perfect treat for the Halloween Season. I had a Halloween party and this was the perfect scary treat!

Ingredients

1 Pack, 7.6 oz	Reese's Minis Unwrapped
1 Pack, 9.9 oz	Reese's Pieces
1 Pack, 11 oz	Brach's Pumpkin Candy Corn
1 Pack, 11 oz	Candy Corn
5 Boxes	Caramel Popcorn or Crunch n' Munch
12 oz	Mini Pretzels
2 Tbsp	Orange Crystal Sprinkles

You Will Need

- Extra Large Serving Bowl
- Serving Cups
- Spoon
- Measuring Cups
- Spatula

Instructions

1 Add 5 boxes of caramel popcorn or Crunch n' Munch to the extra large bowl

2 Add 5 cups of mini pretzels into the bowl

3 Add pumpkin candy corn, candy corn, Reese's Mini Unwrapped and Reese's Pieces

4 Sprinkle the orange spprinkles into the mixture

5 Gently stir with a spatula

6 Spoon into the serving cups

7 Serve and enjoy!

Serafina Alessi

Baking Magic with Serafina the Unicorn Baker 53

SMOOTHIES AND SNACKS

27

Makes 4 servings

Cream Cheese Marshmallow Fluff Fruit Dip

This is healthy and delicious. The fluff might not be healthy, but that's okay, it's dessert! This is simple to make and you do not need to buy this at a grocery store. Lastly, you'll love this for holidays like Memorial Day or the Fourth of July!

Ingredients

7 oz	Marshmallow fluff
18oz Pack	Cream Cheese
1/2 Tsp	Vanilla Extract
1	Fruit Platter (melon, grapes, pineapple, berries)

You Will Need
- Stand Mixer
- Mixing Bowl
- Spoon
- Spatula

Instructions

1. Add 7 ounches of marshmallow fluff into a mixing bowl
2. Add 1 package of cream cheese and 1/2 teaspoon of vanilla extract
3. Place into a stand mixer and mix on low until smooth
4. Pour into a serving bowl
5. Place cut fruit around the perimeter of the bowl

Serve and enjoy!

SMOOTHIES AND SNACKS

28

At-Home Disney Dole Whip

This is good either on a vacation or home. Also, it's great as a dessert to cool off, especially when you get out of the pool!

Makes 4 servings

Ingredients

2 Cups	Frozen Pineapple
1/4 Cup	Coconut Milk (or milk of your choice)
1 Tsp	Lemon Juice
1 Packet	Stevia
2 Pinches	Salt

You Will Need
- Blender
- Serving Bowl
- Measuring Cups
- Spatula
- Teaspoon

Instructions

1 Add all of the contents into a blender

2 Blend until smooth

3 Have a taste, and add an additional stevia packet if you prefer it more sweet

4 Pour contents into a bowl and freeze for 15-20 minutes

Serve and enjoy!

SMOOTHIES AND SNACKS

29

Scary Halloween Protein Pancakes

Perfect and easy to make around Halloween.

Makes 3 servings

Ingredients

3 Scoops	Vanilla Whey Protein Powder
2	Eggs
1/2 Cup	Orange Sprinkles
2 oz	Water
A little	Non-stick Cooking Spray

You Will Need

- Measuring Cup
- Mixing Bowl
- Spatula
- Spoon
- Cooking Pan
- Halloween Cookie Cutouts

Instructions

1 Crack 2 eggs into a large mixing bowl

2 Add 3 scoops of vanilla protein powder into the bowl

3 Add in 2 oz of water and stir the mixture into batter consistency. Add a tiny bit more water if needed

4 Turn the stove on medium heat and spray a pan with non-stick spray,

5 Use a spoon to add mixture in 3-inch cookie size portions

6 After approximately 90 seconds, flip like a pancake, and cook the other side. Continue with the remaining batter

7 Use the cookie cutters to cut the pancakes into the shapes of your choice, then sprinkle with orange sprinkles

Serve and enjoy!

Baking Magic with Serafina the Unicorn Baker

SMOOTHIES AND SNACKS

30

Makes 12 muffins

Oatmeal Breakfast Cups

Turn boring oatmeal into something fabulous! I think this is how my Grandpa should really eat oatmeal.

Ingredients

3 Cups	Old Fashioned Oats
1 Tsp	Baking Powder
1/2 Tsp	Sea Salt
1/4 Tbsp	Cinnamon
4	Eggs
2	Bananas
1 Cup	Milk
3/4 Cup	Honey
1 Tsp	Vanilla Extract
3 Tsp	Cocoa Powder
1/3 Cup	Chocolate Chips

You Will Need

- 2 Large Mixing Bowls
- Measuring Cup
- Measing Spoons
- Muffin Baking Tray
- Cupcake Liners
- Spatula
- Plate
- Whisk

Instructions

1. Preheat the oven to 350°F

2. Pour 3 cups of old fashioned oats into a mixing bowl, then add the baking powder and sea salt

3. In a separate bowl, beat 4 eggs and mash 2 bananas, then add them to the oat mixture

4. Add milk, honey, cinnamon and vanilla extract to the oat mixture and stir

5. Let the mixture sit for 10 minutes

Serafina Alessi

6. Divide the mixture into two equal halves, so we can make one half vanilla and the other half chocolate

7. In one of the bowls, add 3 teaspoons of baking cocoa and 1/3 cup of chocolate chips

8. Line the muffin baking tray with cupcake liners, then fill with the chocolate and vanilla batter

9. Bake for 20 minutes, then remove from the oven and let cool

Serve and enjoy!

Conclusion

And with that, my baking journey came to an end. I hope that this book has inspired you to get in the kitchen and start baking! Whether you're baking with your kids, family, or friends, remember to always have fun and enjoy the process.

Baking has been a huge part of my life and I am so grateful for the memories and experiences it has brought me. I will always cherish the time I spent in the kitchen creating sweet treats and bringing joy to others.

So, I want to leave you with this final thought: baking is not just about making delicious treats, it's about making memories that will last a lifetime. So, keep baking, keep creating, and keep spreading joy to those around you.

Thank you for joining me on this magical baking adventure. I hope you had as much fun as I did!

With love,

Serafina the Unicorn Baker

Don't forget to subscribe to my YouTube channel, Serafina the Unicorn Baker (@serafinatheunicornbaker).

I will be sharing even more baking adventures, tips, and tricks that you won't want to miss. From new recipes to behind-the-scenes footage, my channel is the perfect place for all things unicorn and baking.

www.ingramcontent.com/pod-product-compliance
Lightning Source LLC
Chambersburg PA
CBHW041103070526
44583CB00002B/36